Teaching Handbook for
Revolution in France

Josh Brooman

LONGMAN

All references to attainment targets in this *Handbook* are given using Hi rather than AT. Thus, AT1(a) level 3 becomes Hi/3a

Longman Group UK Limited
Longman House, Burnt Mill, Harlow, Essex, CM20 2JE, England and Associated Companies throughout the World.

First published 1993
ISBN 0 582 10281 2

Set in 11/15pt Bodoni
Prepared for publication
printed and bound by
Longman York Publishing Services

The Publishers' policy is to use paper manufactured from sustainable forests

Designed by: Roger Walton Studio

Contents

1 Introduction

Revolution in France is a teaching and learning resource for a Key Stage 3 supplementary study unit on European history before 1914. The aim of this *Handbook* is to help teachers who have chosen *Revolution in France* to plan and teach the unit and to assess their pupils' attainment in it. To that end, the *Handbook* is organised in the following way.

Chapter 2 General planning issues deals with planning issues which must be considered when preparing a study unit on the French revolutionary and Napoleonic era.

Chapter 3 Notes on the sources provides further information both about the sources and about the approach to historical content in the *Revolution in France* pupils' book.

Chapter 4 Planning a scheme of work suggests some approaches to planning a scheme of work for a course of around eighteen hours of teaching time and outlines a number of classroom activities and tasks related mostly to the text and sources in *Revolution in France**.

Chapter 5 Assessment indicates how the questions and activities in *Revolution in France* might be used to help assess pupils' attainment in the subject.

Chapter 6 Further resources lists a number of readily available books which teachers and pupils might consult, and provides information on a wide variety of other resources.

* The assignments on the photocopyable Copymaster sheets (pages 31–42) can be used to support the activities. Pupils may find some of these assignments easier if the sheets are enlarged when photocopied. This applies particularly to numbers 1a, 1b, 4b, 6a and 6b.

2 General planning issues

The statutory Order for history lays down a number of specific as well as general requirements which must be considered when planning a supplementary study unit on European history.

Relation to the core study units

The first specific requirement of the Order (page 33) is that the supplementary study units in Key Stage 3 'should complement or extend the core study units'. A study unit on the French Revolution and Napoleonic era can achieve this in several ways:

- It could be taught after Core Study Unit 3, The Making of the United Kingdom, in order to provide contrasts and parallels with the central theme of that unit, namely the changing relationships between Crown, Parliament and people in Britain.
- It could be inserted into or taught after Core Study Unit 4, Expansion, Trade and Industry. This would allow contrasts and connections to be made between political and social developments in Britain and Europe during the eighteenth and nineteenth centuries.
- It could be taught in conjunction with, or after, Core Study Unit 1, The Roman Empire, in order to trace the many cultural and ideological links between the Roman Empire and that established by the French Revolutionaries and by Napoleon.

Historical significance

A second specific requirement of the Order is that the unit 'be based on an episode or turning point of major significance' in European history (page 47). It should 'illustrate links between developments in different parts of Europe', and it 'should examine the short- and long-term impact of the episode or turning point'.

Few would disagree that the French revolutionary and Napoleonic era was of major importance in European as well as French history. The Revolution of 1789 had an immediate impact on the political affairs of many European countries, while the era as a whole, 1789–1815, conditioned the political, ideological, social, economic and cultural development of Europe in the first half of the nineteenth century. *Revolution in France* has been written with this European dimension in mind. It not only describes in detail the causes and events of the French Revolution but also shows how, over a long time-span, events which started in France influenced developments in other countries for many years to come.

Perspectives

There is a general requirement that, across the key stage, pupils should be taught history from a range of perspectives: political; economic, technological and scientific; social; religious; and cultural and aesthetic. While there is no requirement to teach from all these perspectives in every single study unit, *Revolution in France* has been written with the PESC formula in mind, as the table opposite shows.

Links with the attainment targets

A general requirement of the Key Stage 3 programme of study is that pupils should have opportunities to develop knowledge, skills and understanding relevant to each of the three attainment targets. Particular opportunities are listed on page 34 of the Order, and teachers are advised in the *Non-Statutory Guidance* to make provision for these when planning study units. As the table on pages 8 and 9 shows, *Revolution in France* can provide pupils with all the required opportunities.

Historical perspectives in *Revolution in France*

	Chapter 1	Chapter 2	Chapter 3	Chapter 4	Chapter 5
Political	The government of France, 15–18 An attempt at reform, 20–21 The Estates General, 21–25	Revolution, 1789, 28–34 The King and the Assembly, 35–44 The Reign of Terror, 45–49	Napoleon the soldier, 52–57 Napoleon the ruler, 57–65	Napoleon conquers Europe, 67–73 Opposition to Napoleon, 74–77 The fall of Napoleon, 78–79	Traces of the revolutionary era, 82–87
Economic technological and scientific	Unequal taxation, 9–11 Financial problems, 19 A *philosophe* at work, 12–13	Inflation and shortages, 43 Economic terror, 47			
Social	French people and their society, 4–6 The three estates, 7 Poverty, 8–9	The *sans culottes*, 42–43		Social change in Napoleonic Europe, 70–71	
Religious	The Calas affair 13–14	The reform of the Church, 36 Terror and the Church, 48	The Concordat and the Catholic Church, 62		
Cultural and aesthetic		Images of the Bastille, 30–32 Engravings, 50–51	The making of a legend, 58–62		Images of revolution, 88–91
	paintings, engravings, drawings, cartoons, sculptures throughout				

		Chapter 1	Chapter 2
Links with AT1	Use words and phrases related to the passing of time	Year, decade	Revolutionary Calendar Reign of Terror
	Investigate different kinds of historical change	Changes in public opinion, 12–14	Reforms of the National Assembly, 35
	Distinguish between features of past societies which changed and those which remained constant	The three estates, 7–8	
	Examine different types of cause and consequence	Causes of the 1789 Revolution: the whole chapter	Results of the Terror, 48–49
	Study the ideas, beliefs and attitudes of people in different societies, relating them to their circumstances	Critics of French society, 12–14,	The *sans culottes*, 42–43
Links with AT2	Identify differences in the ways in which past events have been interpreted		Two views of the *sans culottes*, 42–43 Two views on the nature of the Revolution, 50–51
	Consider reasons why interpretations of the past differ	Opinions about Marie Antoinette, 15–17	Images of the Bastille, 30–32
	Develop an understanding that interpretations of the past can be conveyed in different ways through a variety of media		
Links with AT3	Study a range of historical sources . . .	Sources include contemporary and later paintings, engravings, statistics, journals, memoirs, legal documents.	Sources include contemporary paintings and engravings, diaries, photographs of artefacts
	. . . and comment on their value	Question 2 on sources 20–25	Questions on sources 16 and 17 Questions on sources 25 and 26

	Chapter 3	Chapter 4	Chapter 5
	Napoleon's reforms, 62–65	The Hundred Days Changes in Bonaparte-ruled Europe, 69–71 Questions on page 81 Change and continuity in Napoleonic Europe: the whole chapter	Era of revolution Traces of the revolutionary era, 82–87 Images of revolution, 88–91 Liberalism, nationalism and revolution 1815–48, 83–87
			Legends and myths of revolution, 92–93 Images of revolution, 88–91
	Sources include contemporary and later paintings, memoirs, historians' writings Questions 2–7 about sources 1–14	Sources include contemporary and later paintings and engravings, memoirs and a letter Questions 2–3 about sources 7–12 and 13–14	Sources include letters, memoirs contemporary and later paintings and engravings, photographs of artefacts, and a nursery rhyme Question 7 on page 93 about images of Napoleon in chapters 3–5

Links with other subjects

The Order states that in each key stage pupils should have opportunities to explore links between history and other subjects. Although there is no requirement to do so within each unit, the NCC recommends teachers to identify links in their planning of each unit. *Revolution in France* allows the following links to be made.

Art: Ar2 Knowledge and understanding

The 56 paintings, engravings and etchings reproduced in full colour in *Revolution in France* represent neo-classical and romantic tendencies in art and are the subject of many questions and exercises. They could be used for detailed work on the evaluation of the work of artists and to aid pupils' understanding of our artistic heritage and their appreciation of a variety of other traditions. Specific links in *Revolution in France* are:

Cartoons	8	Engravings	50–51
Images of the Bastille	29–31	Paintings of Napoleon	53–65
Engraving	36	Cartoon and painting	78–79
Storming of the Tuileries	40–41	Images of revolution	88–91
Pictures of *sans culottes*	42–43	Napoleon's coffin	92
Painting of four sisters	46		

Geography: Gg2 Knowledge and understanding of places; Gg4 Human geography; Gg5 Environmental geography

The NCC's *Geography Non-Statutory Guidance* suggests that a geography unit of work could be taught in Year 8 at the same time as a history unit on the French Revolution and Napoleonic era. Specific sections in *Revolution in France* which allow links to be made are:

The flight to Varennes	37	Napoleon's Europe, 1810	70–71
The crisis of 1793	44	Europe in 1815	85
Impact of the Terror	47		
Napoleon's campaigns	54		

Mathematics; Ma2 Number; Ma4 Shape and space

One of the legacies of the French Revolutionary era is the metric system, adopted over the past two hundred years by nearly every country in the world. Less long-lasting, but also of mathematical interest, was the Revolutionary Calendar used in France from 1793 to 1 January 1806. Specific pages in *Revolution in France* which could be used for work in number and measurement are:

The cost of living	9	The Revolutionary Calendar	48

Religious education

Religious and clerical problems helped cause the French Revolution and religious dissension helped to make it a violent revolution. The four sections in *Revolution in France* specifically concerned with these issues are:

The Calas affair	13–14	Terror and the Church	48
Reform of the Church	36	The Concordat	62

Cross-curricular themes

Citizenship

French people and society	4–8	Declaration of the Rights of Man and the Citizen	83–84
Taxation	9–10		

Economic and industrial understanding

Poverty	8–9	Financial problems	19
Taxation	9–10		

Historical sources

The Order stipulates that pupils should have opportunities across the key stage to use a variety of historical sources, including documents and printed sources; artefacts; pictures and photographs; music; buildings and sites; and computer-based materials. *Revolution in France* contains a very wide range of such sources.

Documents and printed sources	
Memoirs	55, 56, 62, 73, 76, 77, 86
Diaries	16, 17, 32
Letters	18, 85
Contemporary books and newspapers	8, 45
Legal documents	8, 18, 35, 55
Political documents	18, 23, 87
Historians' writings	16, 17, 31, 59
Photographs of artefacts	
Model of a guillotine	45
A Revolutionary Calendar	48
A wooden mural	83
A tricolour flag	84
A polystyrene statue	91
Pictures	
Contemporary paintings, engravings and etchings	5, 6, 12, 13, 14, 15, 16, 19, 25, 29, 30, 31, 33, 34, 36, 38, 39, 40, 41, 42, 43, 49, 50, 51, 58, 60, 63, 64-65, 72, 73, 74, 78, 87, 88, 89, 90
19th century academic paintings	17, 20, 22, 24, 46, 53, 56, 61, 68–9, 77, 79, 80, 86, 92
Maps	37, 44, 47, 54, 70–1, 85
Diagrams	19
Pictures of buildings	
The palace of Versailles	15
Marie Antoinette's village	16
The Statue of Liberty	90
The Arc de Triomphe	93
Music	
A lullaby	93

3 Notes on the sources

The notes in this section of the *Handbook* have three purposes:

- to provide further information about the sources – information which could not be included in the pupils' book without overburdening it;
- to give teachers more details about the subject matter for use in their presentations of topics;
- to help answer questions that pupils might ask about what they have read.

The notes relate only to material in the pupils' book and are not intended as a broader commentary on the history of the period. Teachers wanting more general treatments of the period are referred to Part 6 of this *Handbook* (see page 55).

Chapter 1 France before the Revolution

Four families (sources 1–4, page 5)

Each of these four paintings is full of details which reveal the social class of the family. Pupils should have little difficulty in discerning basic features which indicate poverty or wealth (e.g. furniture and furnishings; flooring; clothing, wigs and shoes; toys and pets). Less obvious indications to which attention may need to be drawn are listed below.

Source 2

The bed in the background on the right and the fireplace on the left (with cooking utensils just out of this enlarged picture) suggests that the family was living in one room. The picture is called 'Paternal love' and the artist intended it as an ideal of loving family life. He presumably did not therefore consider living in one room to be an obstacle to family harmony.

Source 4

The blue sashes (*cordon bleu*) worn by the men indicate that they were members of an aristocratic order, the Order of the Holy Spirit. The Duke's son is also wearing the badge of the Order. (He is drinking his chocolate in the customary eighteenth-century way of drinking coffee or chocolate – from a saucer.)

Illustrations from the *Encyclopédie* (page 6)

These show, from top left, peasants using recently invented farming machinery to cultivate the soil; butchers slaughtering livestock; a bakery; bee-keepers; a wig-making workshop; a soldier presenting arms. The *Encyclopédie* was published between 1751 and 1772, and consisted of 17 volumes of text and eleven volumes of finely engraved illustrations. Because they are so detailed and realistic these give superb insights into many aspects of eighteenth-century French life.

Poverty (pages 8–9)

Source 9, taken from the records of a charity organisation, consists of examples of needy people who asked it for charity. The examples were collected to show its staff how to distinguish between the 'deserving' and 'undeserving' poor. These may therefore not provide a typical picture of poverty in one place at one time.

In source 10, the reference to 'rent of a fourth- or fifth-floor room' is revealing. The floor on which a family lived was a clear indicator of the occupants' wealth and social status. The wealthiest lived on the ground floor. Wealth and status decreased with each floor, with poverty being common on the sixth or seventh floors and in attics and garrets. The reference to a fourth- or fifth-floor room in source 10 was therefore perhaps meant to suggest a family of modest means, but not a poverty-stricken one.

The 4-pound loaf listed in source 11 was the standard French loaf at this time. (See the loaves in the basket on the floor in source 5.) Made in large parts of the country from a variety of grains and including a good deal of bran, its heavy consistency made it difficult to digest, according to some contemporary accounts. White bread made from wheat flour was common in the wheat-growing areas around Paris, but crusty white loaves such as the baguette, which we associate with France today, were unknown. The baguette was a Viennese import dating from the 1840s.

Exemptions from tax in the 1780s (page 10)
The *taille* was originally a war tax payable by anyone who did not do military service. Nobles, originally the warrior class, were presumed automatically to do such service and were therefore exempt – even if they never undertook it. The clergy were exempt on the grounds that their calling forbade them to fight. Over the years, exemption was also acquired by certain office-holders in law courts and local government. Townspeople also traditionally paid less than their full share. With so many people thus exempt, the burden of the *taille* fell most heavily on the peasants.

The *capitation* and the *twentieths* were introduced around the start of the eighteenth century, with the intention that there should be no exemptions. However, nobles and clergy soon found all sorts of ways of evading payment: for example, by falsifying their income declarations, by intimidating the tax collector, by mounting protests in law courts, and so on.

Feudal rights and dues (page 11)
Probably the most hated of the feudal rights were the rights of the warren and the dovecote. Since the Middle Ages, most landlords had kept pigeons in dovecotes as a source of food (squab meat). Selective breeding of pigeons had also led to their use for racing and for carrying messages. (Pigeons, for example, would relay news to Britain of Napoleon's defeat at Waterloo.) Rabbits were kept both for their fur and for eating, especially the latter because they were considered as fish for religious purposes and could therefore be eaten on meatless days in the Catholic calendar.

Peasants hated the landlords' rights to keep rabbits and pigeons because of the damage they often did to crops. One result of the Revolution of 1789 was the disappearance of many warrens and dovecotes. The number of dovecotes declined further in the nineteenth century as farmers came to realise that feeding grain to birds was less profitable than using it to make bread. The release of dovecote populations eventually resulted in the huge flocks of feral pigeons that have lived in towns and cities ever since.

Portrait of the Lavoisiers (source 15, page 13)
The dominant figure in the portrait is Anne-Marie Lavoisier who was a pupil of the artist, David, and whose portfolio can be seen propped on a chair in the background. She drew the illustrations for her husband's famous work *Traité élémentaire de chimie* and helped him in his experiments. The scientific instrument on the table in front of them is a 'gasometer'. Mercury from the flask on the right was poured through the first tube on top of the gasometer in order to displace gas

in it. The gas was collected in the large glass balloon on the floor which was connected to the other tube on the gasometer. The copper instrument behind the glass balloon is a hydrometer.

Antoine Lavoisier was not only a scientist. He was also a financier who had bought a franchise from the King to collect taxes. Being a 'tax farmer' made him very unpopular and he was executed along with other tax farmers in 1794.

Breaking on the wheel (source 16, page 14)
This was the most extreme form of punishment regularly used by French courts. Around 30 people were broken on the wheel each year during the 1780s, 21 of them in 1789. The more usual form of capital punishment was hanging, with an average of 50 a year going to the gallows, and 84 in 1789. Other severe forms of punishment included life sentences in the galleys or workhouse (100 per year on average), banishment (41 in 1789), and a variety of corporal punishments: flogging, branding and the iron collar.

The royal debt (page 19)
By today's standards, the government's spending was very modest. Its spending of 633.1 million livres was equivalent to around £1200 million sterling in today's prices. Pupils could contrast this with the British government's current spending of around £25,000 million a year on education alone.

The first meeting of the Estates General (source 35, page 24)
This historical reconstruction of the scene, painted for its fiftieth anniversary, shows Jacques Necker, Director-General of Finances, addressing the Estates General on the subject of the financial crisis. The artist has given prominence to the deputies of the third estate seated in the foreground, although nobody at the time of this meeting knew that the third estate would shortly dominate events. Pupils might spot, in the third row, the only person in the room not wearing a wig and the formal dress required of deputies. He was Michel Gérard, the only peasant to be elected to the Estates General, and who created a sensation by appearing in rustic clothes.

The Tennis Court Oath (source 36, page 25)
The tennis court was a Real Tennis court, larger than but not unlike a squash court. It is doubtful whether David was present at the swearing of the oath, but whether he was or not, the painting was not meant as a realistic depiction of the scene. In actuality, the deputies were seated calmly in two groups on either side of a table facing the wall on the right. In David's picture the table is in the centre of the

court and the deputies are portrayed as a single united group making operatic gestures of excitement, awe and profound feeling. The figures are grouped to suggest various acts of revolution. For example, the three central figures in the foreground are representatives of the regular clergy, the secular clergy and of France's Protestants: their embrace symbolises the principles of religious tolerance and unity. Only one figure in the painting does not in some way symbolise unity and revolutionary ardour. He is Martin Dauch, the only deputy who refused the oath, shown with his arms folded on the far right of the picture.

Chapter 2 Revolution and Terror, 1789–1794

The Marquis de Sade's journal (page 32)

The Marquis de Sade, from whose journal sources 5 and 6 are taken, spent 28 years of his life in prison for sexual offences. Following an orgy in 1772 with four prostitutes and his manservant, in which one of the prostitutes fell ill from eating aphrodisiac sweets, de Sade was sentenced to death for sodomy and poisoning. He escaped, fled, and spent the next five years dodging the police and army before being re-arrested in 1777. The death sentence was commuted but he was imprisoned by *lettre de cachet* at the request of his own family. The pornographic novels which he wrote while a prisoner in the Bastille and at Vincennes described masochism as well as the 'sadism' for which he is the eponym.

As sources 5 and 6 suggest, de Sade led a comfortable existence in prison. This was because prisoners then had to pay for their own upkeep, and he was wealthy.

Elixir of Garus was a liqueur, named after its inventor, used for medicinal purposes. The 's' is sounded.

The women march to Versailles (page 34)

There is no evidence that Marie Antoinette said (on this or any other occasion) 'Let them eat cake' when told that the hungry Parisians could not afford bread. (*'S'ils n'ont pas de pain qu'ils mangent de la brioche.'*) The charge that she did so was just one of dozens of calumnies against her invented by popular opinion between 1789 and her execution in 1793. The true origin of the phrase is not known for certain, however. Some authorities attribute it to Jean-Jacques Rousseau, writing in his *Confessions* about a time in 1740 when he was a family tutor in an aristocratic household: 'I remember the substitute suggested by a great princess who had been told that the peasants had no bread and replied "let them eat cake (brioche)".' An alternative source was suggested by Marie Antoinette's brother-in-law, Louis XVIII, who wrote in 1823 that it was said by Marie Thérèse (1638–83), wife of Louis XIV: 'Why don't they eat pastry?' (*'Que ne mangent-ils de la croûte de pâté?'*)

In the picture of the women returning from Versailles (source 8), the heads being carried on poles were those of the two bodyguards killed during the assault on the palace. The other objects impaled on poles are loaves of bread.

The storming of the Tuileries (page 41)
Johann Zoffany, who painted source 15, 'Plundering the king's cellars' was a German-born artist who had lived mainly in Britain after leaving Frankfurt in 1760. He was in Britain when he painted this in the summer of 1794. The French armies at that time were winning the Revolutionary wars and many people in Britain feared a French invasion. The painting, which was made into a popular engraving in 1795, may therefore have been a form of propaganda, warning of the horrors to be expected in the event of occupation by the French.

Cartoon (source 16, page 42)
This cartoon was selected to illustrate the very powerful emotions aroused in Britain by news of the violence of the *sans culottes*, and to allow comparisons to be made with the interpretation in source 17, painted by a French admirer of the *sans culottes*. It is a violent and potentially disturbing image, and pupils might be reassured if it is pointed out that it does not depict a real event. Comparisons could be made with twentieth-century cartooning traditions to show pupils how cartoonists use exaggeration and distortion to make a point.

The guillotine (page 45)
There was, unsurprisingly, fierce controversy at the time about the effects of sudden decapitation on the victim's mind and body. It was common practice for the executioner to hold up the severed head for the crowd to see, and witnesses sometimes reported seeing eye movements, convulsions, the grinding of teeth and blushing on the faces of some heads. In experiments on corpses, doctors were also able to induce convulsions in bodies and heads by touching the exposed spinal cord. Stories, presumably apocryphal, circulated of victims settling the dispute by giving friends prearranged signals, such as a wink, after the blade had fallen. Such stories fuelled the argument between those who believed that execution by guillotine was painless and therefore humane, and those who believed that victims knew exactly what had happened to them. The controversy is described by Ludmilla

Jordanova in 'Medical mediations: mind, body and the guillotine', *History Workshop Journal* 28, Autumn 1989.

The Revolutionary Calendar (page 48)

The Revolutionary Calendar is one of history's great might-have-beens. Whereas the metric system of weights and measures, introduced during the Revolution, has since spread all over the world, the metric calendar lasted for only fifteen years and no trace of it now survives.

The Revolutionary Calendar was introduced in 1793 and replaced the traditional Gregorian calendar in its entirety. Years were renumbered, with 1792 becoming Year I (to imply that the birth of the French Republic in that year was more important than the birth of Christ).

The year was divided into ten equal months of thirty days, each named after the seasons and phenomena of nature. The months of autumn all ended in *-aire*, those of winter in *-ôse*, of spring in *-al* and of summer in *-or*. At the end of the year were five (in leap years 6) extra days called *sans culotte* days (re-named complementary days after 1795). Each month was divided into three *décades*, each *décade* into days lasting ten hours, each hour into 100 minutes and each minute into 100 seconds. The days were named after the ordinal numbers, from *primidi* up to *décadi*. To take the place of saints' days, which were all abolished, each fifth day (*quintidi*) was named after a domestic animal and each *décadi* after a farming implement. All other days were named after grains, fields, trees, roots, flowers, fruits or plants.

The calendar was used in France, its colonies, sister republics and annexed territories from October 1793 until its abolition on 1 January 1806. It failed to survive for many reasons. First, nobody apart from extreme revolutionaries had particularly disliked the old Gregorian calendar, so there was no popular demand for its replacement in the first place. Second, however rational and logical it may have been, it did not seem to most people to be an improvement on the Gregorian calendar. Nobody, for example, liked having every tenth day rather than seventh day as their weekly day off work. Third, it was difficult to use: not only was it intellectually difficult for many people to grasp, but also the fact that nothing at all was left of the old calendar meant that they had no temporal landmarks to use as bearings. Without, for example, Christmas, Easter or any saints' days, and with such innovations as a ten-day week, people's sense of time was seriously disturbed. And fourth, it wasn't quite as rational and logical as its inventors claimed. The agricultural and natural events described by the names of the months applied only to the Paris region. It may have made sense to Parisians to call December 'the month of snow', but not to the people of, say, Marseille, where it hardly ever snowed. Finally, the old calendar was closely bound up with religion. With Christmas, Easter, Sundays and over a hundred saints' days to be observed in the year, the calendar was one of the ways in which the Church exercised social control and regulated social life. Abolition of the calendar was one of the grounds for dispute between the Church and the revolutionary government, so when Napoleon reached agreement with the Pope in the Concordat of 1802, it became increasingly difficult for his government to resist popular demands for the restoration of the old calendar.

Full details of the Revolutionary Calendar are shown in the table on Copymaster 4, page 36 of this *Handbook*.

Chapter 3 The rise of Napoleon

The Battle of Rivoli (source 1, page 53)

The Battle of Rivoli (14–15 January 1797) was the final battle in a French campaign to capture the strategic city of Mantua. During the battle Napoleon was surrounded several times by the Austrians and a number of horses were shot from under him. For Napoleon, as for the rest of the French forces, the battle was a closely fought one. Pupils could consider how far the picture reflects this.

Map of Napoleon's campaigns (source 2, page 54)

The arrows pointing to the Netherlands, with the caption 'conquered 1795–1798', should not be red: these were French conquests, but not by Napoleon.

The Battle of Marengo (source 7, pages 58–59)

General Lejeune, who painted this, fought in the Battle of Marengo, so his painting could be considered from some points of view as a most useful source of evidence about it. From one point of view, however, it might be considered unrealistic. If this military historian is right, it is questionable whether Lejeune could have seen much of it:

> *After the first few discharges, clouds of black powder smoke, together with the dust raised by thousands of men, horses and wheels, created quite literally 'the fog of battle'. Men in action saw little. Rifleman Harris remembered that after several firings he was 'enveloped in the smoke I created, and the cloud which hung about me from the continued fire of my comrades was such that I could see nothing . . . but the red flash of my own piece'.*
>
> Gunther Rothenburg, *The Art of Warfare in the Age of Napoleon*

In addition, note how clean all the soldiers are. Uniforms are bright and uncreased. Faces are white, although musket-fire burned and blackened the faces of soldiers firing them. The wounded are not bleeding. On the other hand, the painting contains unusual details which suggest close knowledge of battlefield conditions. Note, for example, a dead soldier robbed of his uniform, a dog hit by a cannon-ball, a soldier committing suicide, a black soldier driving a team of horses.

Napoleon crossing the Saint-Bernard (source 9, page 60)
The carvings on the rocks in the foreground compare Bonaparte with Hannibal, who crossed the Alps with an army in 218 BC, and to Charlemagne (Karolus Magnus) who crossed in AD 773.

The re-establishment of worship (source 13, page 63)
On the church is an inscription surviving from the Reign of Terror: 'The French People recognise the Supreme Being and the Immortality of the Soul', a reference to the non-Christian Cult of the Supreme Being introduced by the Committee of Public Safety in 1794.

The Consecration of the Emperor (source 14, pages 64–65)
The painting is true to life in every detail but one. Napoleon's mother, shown seated in an arch at the very centre of the painting, did not attend. Pupils could be asked to think about why David invented this one detail.

The people portrayed in the foreground of the painting are, from left to right: Napoleon's brothers Joseph and Louis Bonaparte, Napoleon's sisters Caroline Murat, Pauline Borghese and Elisa Bacchiochi, his sisters-in-law Hortense (wife of Louis Bonaparte, holding the hand of little Prince Charles) and Julie (wife of Joseph Bonaparte). The Empress's train is held by Madame de la Rochefoucauld and Madame de la Valette. Behind them, left to right, are Louis-Philippe de Ségur (Grand Master of Ceremonies) and Marshals Bessières, Moncey, Sérurier and Murat (the latter carrying the Empress's honours on a cushion). Sitting behind Napoleon is Pope Pius VII surrounded by cardinals and bishops. To the right of the Pope are ministers Lebrun, Cambacérès, Marshal Berthier (holding the orb) and Talleyrand. The choirboys are staring at Eugène Beauharnais' sword.

Chapter 4 Napoleon and Europe

The Surrender at Ulm (source 1, pages 68–69)

An Hi2 exercise could be developed by comparing source 1, painted 28 years after the battle, with the following assessment of Napoleon's victory by a British military historian:

> *Ulm . . . was a success that only just escaped being a disaster, and even then escaped largely because of the incompetence of the enemy. For – as always – Bonaparte was working on the narrowest of margins. As he himself acknowledged . . . after Mack's surrender 'had the army suffered some reverse, the lack of magazines would have led us into the gravest difficulties . . . '. Troops exhausted by ceaseless marching would arrive at their camping ground, so an eyewitness writes, 'having eaten nothing and finding no supplies waiting for them'. Hunger, fatigue and the icy weather led to 'insubordination, indiscipline and marauding', according to the same officer; 'except in the Russian campaign I have never suffered so much or seen so much disorder'.*
>
> Corelli Barnett, *Bonaparte*, Allen and Unwin, 1978, p.110

In the valley of the shadow of death (source 13, page 78)

The speech bubbles 'Remember Junot' and 'Remember Dupont' are references to two of Napoleon's less fortunate generals. Junot, a general by the age of thirty and tipped for a Marshal's baton after his conquest of Portugal in 1807, suffered a series of defeats and serious wounds between 1808 and 1812. Soon after becoming governor of the Illyrian Provinces in 1813 he became insane and was stripped of all his offices – upon which he killed himself by jumping out of a window. General Dupont's initially brilliant military career also ended in disgrace. A force of Spanish guerillas and regular troops surrounded his entire force of 30,000 men in 1808 and took them all prisoner. Dupont was allowed to return to France but was disgraced by Napoleon on arrival.

The Lethean Ditch in the foreground is the mythical river Lethe in the underworld whose waters caused drinkers to forget their past. The other river, of course, is the Styx. The moon at top of the picture shows 'British influence' waxing and 'French influence' waning.

The French Campaign (source 14, page 79)

Ernest Meissonier, who painted this, was one of the most successful academic painters of the nineteenth century. He spent a great deal of time researching his subjects and painted them from dozens of prepared sketches. His paintings sold for colossal sums of money.

Chapter 5 The legacy of the revolutionary era

The 'Declaration of the Rights of Man' (source 1, page 83)

The Declaration is shown here painted on a wooden panel. As well as the text it contains several common revolutionary symbols. At the top is the all-seeing eye of reason. Liberty, the figure on the left, is not only breaking the chains of despotism but is also shrugging off the mantle of despotism – a cloak with the royal family's fleur-de-lys emblem on it. In the centre of the panel, dividing the two columns of text, is a *fasces* (a bundle of sticks tied around a spear), the symbol of authority carried in front of magistrates in Ancient Rome as they entered court (and later adopted by the Italian Fascists in the twentieth century).

Above the *fasces* is a Phrygian cap, also known as the Cap of Liberty or the *bonnet rouge*. This was modelled on the Phrygian cap worn by slaves who gained their freedom in ancient times, and was commonly worn by *sans culottes* as a symbol of liberty.

The tricolour flag (source 2, page 84)

This was created in 1789 when Lafayette, commander of the National Guard, combined the traditional colours of the city of Paris, red and blue, with the traditional white of the Bourbon monarchy. The resulting tricolour symbolised the unity of the king and people.

Images of revolution (pages 88–91)

In French, revolutionary ideas and terms mostly have the female gender (e.g. *la liberté, la République, l'égalité, la fraternité, la nature, la force*) because the French language, like Latin, describes abstract entities as female. The allegorical figures such as Marianne, which the revolutionaries created to represent their principles, were thus all women.

The Statue of Liberty (sources 12 and 13, pages 90 and 91)

This was the suggestion of a French historian, Edouard de Laboulaye. Work on it began in 1875 under the direction of a French sculptor, Frédéric Auguste Bartholdi. It was originally intended to commemorate the 100th anniversary of American independence but was not finished until 1886. It later became a symbol of the liberty that the USA supposedly offered to migrants arriving from Europe. Emma Lazarus's poem, 'The New Colossus', carved at the base of the statue, captured this sentiment: 'Give me your tired, your poor, your huddled masses yearning to be free'.

Liberty leading the people (source 10, page 89)

There may be a true story behind this allegorical painting. An anonymous pamphlet published in France in 1831, *Un fait inconnu de Juillet 1830*, states that Delacroix based the painting on the true story of a poor laundry girl named Anne-Charlotte who, dressed only in a petticoat, went in search of her brother Antoine, missing after joining street fighting on 27 July. She eventually found his corpse, naked and with ten bullet wounds in the chest where he had been shot by government troops for carrying weapons. Anne-Charlotte swore to kill ten soldiers in revenge. She had shot nine and was reloading her musket to kill the tenth when a Captain of Lancers killed her with his sabre.

Whether or not the story was true, it seems likely that Delacroix based this scene on its broad outlines, with Liberty portrayed as Anne-Charlotte and the half-naked corpse in the foreground being her brother. The man with a top hat and musket is not, as is sometimes claimed, Delacroix himself, but Etienne Arago, a republican theatre director who took part in the fighting. The boy brandishing the guns on the right is typical of the street urchins who took part in most street disturbances and of whom four were killed in the 1830 revolution. The other figures, dead and alive, are artisans. The picture thus shows a wide cross section of society – bourgeois and working class, male and female, young and old – uniting in the cause of revolution.

4 Planning a scheme of work

This section of the *Handbook* contains ideas and suggestions for planning a scheme of work on the era of the French Revolution and Napoleon, using this *Handbook* in conjunction with the *Revolution in France* pupils' book.

Length of the unit

The Order states that supplementary study units should make demands comparable to those of a core unit, in historical knowledge, understanding and skills. With this requirement in mind, the scheme of work outlined here is based on a maximum of 18 hours of teaching time, supplemented by homework.

Focus

The focus suggested for the unit is to show the importance of the French Revolution and Napoleon in the history of Europe. This can be approached through four basic themes:

- The causes of the French Revolution
- The changes that the Revolution brought about in France
- The spread of revolutionary ideas in Europe under Napoleonic rule
- The consequences of the revolutionary and Napoleonic era for Europe

Key questions

Each of the four themes can be approached through several key questions:

The causes of the French Revolution
What was France like before 1789?
Why did many French people want change by 1789?

The changes that the Revolution brought about in France
What was so important about the events of 1789?
What were the revolutionaries trying to achieve?
Why did the revolutionaries abolish the monarchy and kill the King?
Did the revolutionaries go too far during the Reign of Terror?

The spread of revolutionary ideas under Napoleonic rule
How did Napoleon come to power in France?
How did Napoleon gain (and lose) control of much of Europe?
What changes did Napoleon make in Europe?

The consequences of the revolutionary and Napoleonic era
What were the main ideas of the era?
How did these ideas go on influencing events after the era was over?

Concepts

The sophistication of the concepts involved in the unit will obviously depend on the age and abilities of the pupils. Some basic concepts that pupils are likely to encounter when studying this topic are listed below. (The listing of these concepts here is not intended to imply that pupils should or even could acquire an understanding of them through this study unit alone. The development of conceptual understanding and skill is something to be done across the whole key stage.)

Concepts which reinforce those required for understanding the core study units

government	revolution
parliament	reform
Church	class
monarchy	feudalism
republic	nobility
treaty	peasantry

(see page 35 of the Order)

Concepts associated with the attainment targets

era	change
change	interpretation
cause	myth
consequence	image
motive	evidence

Other concepts arising from the subject matter

bourgeoisie	estates
coup	liberalism
nationalism	liberty

Teaching and learning activities

A number of classroom activities and teaching and learning methods are outlined in the remainder of this section of the *Handbook*. They follow the chapter order of *Revolution in France* and are mostly related to the sources and other material in it. Some of the activities could, however, be adapted for use in other contexts.

Introductory session

The aim of this session is to help pupils engage with the subject by locating it in time and place. This could be done with any or all of the following familiarisation activities:

1 Do the map exercise on Copymaster sheet 1 of this *Handbook* (see pages 31 and 32).

2 What do the following have in common?

Trafalgar Square Maida Vale Waterloo Station

(Places in London named after British victories in the Napoleonic wars)

Nelson's Column Wellington boots

(Named after British commanders in the Napoleonic wars)

Guerillas pigeons the metric system

(Things that spread as a result of the Revolution and Napoleonic wars)

3 Give pupils an overview of the study unit with a slide presentation of the main events of the revolutionary era, then fill in a 'how much of the story can you remember?' sheet.

What was France like before the Revolution?

1 Introduce the structure of French society with an exercise using sources 1–4 on page 5 of *Revolution in France*. Divide the class into

four groups and assign one picture to each group. Working singly or collaboratively, pupils spend five minutes jotting down notes about the lives of the people portrayed in 'their' picture. Then, in a short whole-class session, pupils from each group tell the other groups what they have gathered from the picture they have studied.

2 Elaborate on the structure of society using the material on pages 7–8 about the three estates of French society, centring it around the picture activity on page 8.

Use sources 10 and 11 on page 9 of *Revolution in France* and Copymaster sheet 2, page 33, in this *Handbook* to investigate the subject of poverty.

Finish the session by establishing the unfairness of taxes and feudal dues (sources 12 and 13 on pages 10–11).

3 Introduce the problems of French government with a do-it-yourself quiz game. After reading pages 15, 18 and 19, pupils in groups make up a series of statements about the government of France. Each statement must contain one factual error. One group then reads out its statements to another group which must identify as many errors as possible, then *vice versa*. The group which spots the most errors wins.

Why did many French people want change by 1789?

1 Approach the idea that some people wanted a change of government through the subject of Marie Antoinette's unpopularity, using sources 20 to 25 as the basis of the Hi2 activity on page 17.

The unpopularity of the government could also be tackled through page 18 – the use and abuse of power.

2 Source 34 on page 23 is a useful way of investigating why many people wanted social change.

3 Activity 1 on page 26 of *Revolution in France* can be used by pupils to review what they have learned about France before the Revolution.

What was so important about 1789?

The idea of 1789 being important could be introduced by referring to the annual 14 July celebrations in France (held every year since 1789), to the building of the Eiffel Tower for the 1889 centenary and to the recent 1989 bicentenary celebrations.

The focus of this session could be on images created of the storming of the Bastille, using the text, sources 1–6 and questions on pages 29–32 of *Revolution in France*.

Finish the session by drawing together the ways in which France was changed by revolutionary events in 1789, using Copymaster sheet 3 (see page 34).

What were the revolutionaries trying to achieve?

1 Introduce the idea that the revolutionaries of 1789 were trying to achieve reforms. It may first be necessary to establish the concept of reform by discussing hypothetical reforms in a familiar situation. For example, which of the following at school would be a reform and which just a change?

- The classrooms are repainted during the summer holiday
- A dress code is introduced for pupils
- The netball team beats Grange Hill for the first time in ten years
- A 'continental day' timetable is introduced
- etc. etc. . . .)

2 Study the reforms of the National Assembly in source 9 and do exercise 2 on page 35 of *Revolution in France*.

3 Focus on the reform of the Church as the most contentious and difficult of the reforms. Source 10 on page 36 could be used to introduce the idea of anti-clericalism. To help pupils understand why so many people remained loyal to the Church, point out some of the mechanisms by which the Church maintained social and cultural control: for example, religious services and ceremonies, observance of saints' days (over a hundred a year), personal names (Catholics always took saints' names), confession, religious censorship, the tithe, the physical presence of the church (usually the largest building/s in a town, visible for miles around).

Why did the revolutionaries abolish the monarchy and kill the King?

Pages 37–42 have been written as a continuous exposition to explain the growing conflict between the King and the revolutionaries. The task of working out reasons for the downfall of the monarchy could be divided between groups, with each group preparing an explanation of the following factors:

- Louis' dislike of the reforms of the Church
- The flight to Varennes
- The Brunswick Manifesto
- The storming of the Tuileries

Did the revolutionaries go too far during the Reign of Terror?
This could be the subject of a class exhibition, with groups preparing wall displays or posters on each of the following:

- the *sans culottes*
- the guillotine
- the Revolutionary Calendar
- terror in the provinces

Copymaster sheets 4 and 5 (see pages 36–39) can be used to support pupils' investigations into these topics.

How did Napoleon come to power in France?
This question can be dealt with very much in outline. Using for information pages 52–57 and 62–65 of *Revolution in France*, pupils could do Review activity 1 on page 66.

If time allows, questions 2 to 7 on page 66 could also be used for assessment of Hi3 in connection with Napoleon's rise to power.

How did Napoleon gain control of much of Europe?
The aim of this question is to establish the basic geography of Napoleon's conquests, not the military details of how he did it. One way of doing this is to use Copymaster sheet 6 of this *Handbook* (see pages 40 and 41) in conjunction with page 67 of *Revolution in France*.

What changes did Napoleon make in Europe?
Using the information and the map on pages 70–71, pupils could find six features of Bonaparte rule common to the states coloured orange.

What were the main ideas of the revolutionary and Napoleonic era?
1 The concepts of liberty and equality could be introduced by reference to present-day rights and freedoms, using Copymaster sheet 7, page 42 of this *Handbook*, as a familiarisation exercise.

2 The concept of nationalism in Europe can be introduced through the map on page 85 of the *Revolution in France* pupils' book. Using tracing paper, pupils could draw new borders onto the map of Europe along the lines shown by the different colours, then describe five major ways in which a 'nationalist' Europe would have been different from the Europe restored in 1815.

How did these ideas go on influencing events after the Revolution was over?
The section 'Images of revolution' on pages 88–91 of *Revolution in France* has been written to show how, over a long period of time, one of the central ideas of the revolutionary era – that of liberty – spread to many parts of the world.

Europe before the French Revolution

Copymaster sheet 1a

Look carefully at map 1 below, then compare it with map 2 of Europe today on sheet 1b. In the space at the bottom of map 2, write down all the differences you can see between Europe then and now.

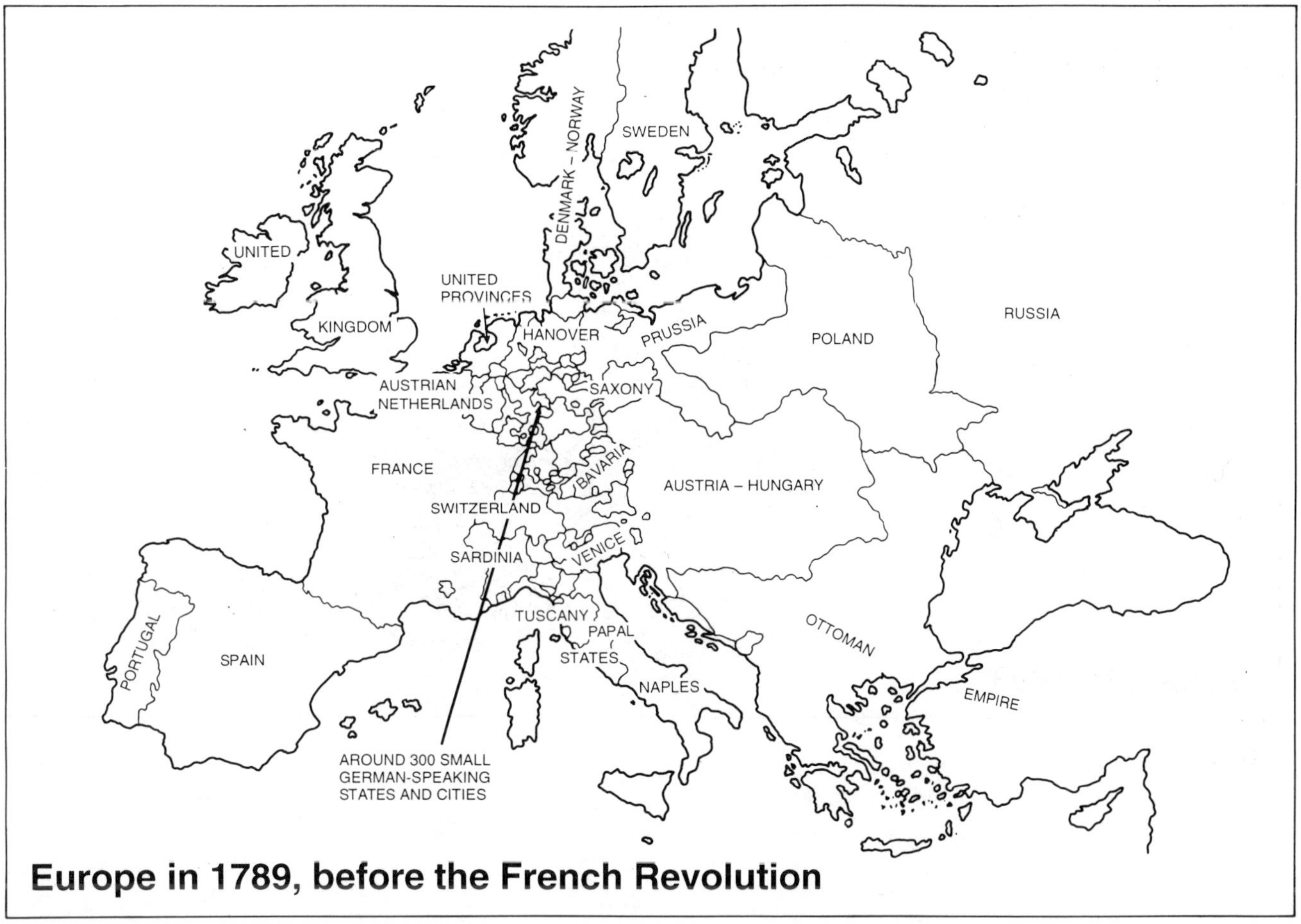

Map 1

Europe before the French Revolution Copymaster sheet 1b

Map 2

Poverty

Copymaster sheet 2

This activity is designed to help you understand some of the problems facing poor French people before 1789. You will need to look at page 9 of your book while you do it.

Your task is to work out how much it would cost to feed an average working family for one week. You have just under 100 *sous* (around £10) to spend. First read this information about what people ate at that time, then answer the questions beneath:

The average working family of five consumed at least 4 pounds of bread each day. They usually had little else to eat. If they did have anything with their bread, it was usually a broth called pot-au-feu. This was made by slowly stewing beef with vegetables (e.g. beans, rice, lentils) in a large pot which stayed on the stove for a week or more, adding water to replace the broth they took from it. They drank wine or water with wine (never plain water because it was polluted) or coffee.

1. Look at source 11 on page 9 of your book and write down how much this would cost:

Bread for one week	________________	sous
Ingredients for pot-au-feu for one week:		
1 pound of beef	________________	sous
1 pound rice or other vegetable	________________	sous
Wine (1 litre bottle) a day	________________	sous
Coffee (1 pound would last a week)	________________	sous

2. You have around 100 *sous* a week to spend on food. How much more than this would it cost to give your family the food listed above?

3. You can't afford to give your family the food listed above. You will have to spend less on other things if you are going to feed them. Here are some suggestions for spending less, based on sources 10 and 11. For each suggestion make a note of any disadvantages of doing it.

Suggested saving	**Disadvantages**
Don't pay your rent	________________________
Cut down on heating	________________________
Buy fewer clothes	________________________
Cut down on things like soap, candles, or lamp oil	________________________
Refuse to pay your capitation tax	________________________
Eat less food	________________________
Other?	________________________

4. What have you decided? Why? How will this affect the way you live?

Events and changes in 1789 — Copymaster sheet 3a

1. Look at the four events of 1789 shown on the map below. Put each event into its correct place on the time-line on sheet 3b.
2. At the bottom of sheet 3b is a list of changes that resulted from these events. Match each change to the event that led to it and write it onto the time-line.

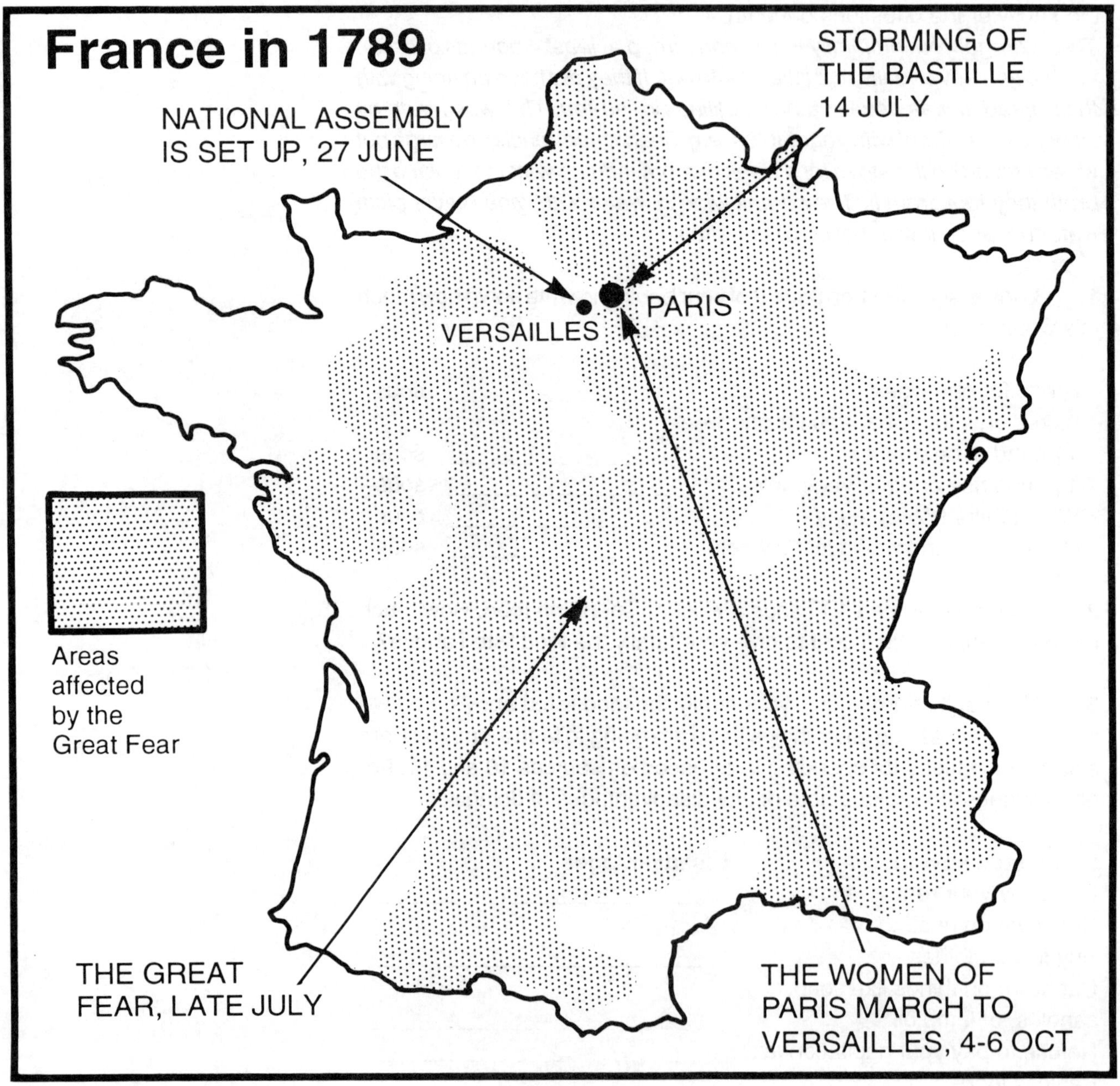

1789 Events

Copymaster sheet 3b

January

February

March

April

May

June

July

August

September

October

November

December

The King and his family had to leave Versailles to live in Paris where the people could keep a watch on them

Nobles gave up their feudal rights and dues

The people of Paris set up their own military force (National Guard) and city government (Paris Commune)

The King was no longer an absolute monarch: he had to share his power

The Revolutionary Calendar

Copymaster sheet 4a

Look at the information panel below. Then, on sheet 4b:

1. Write the months of the Christian calendar into the spaces on disc 1. Start in the 9 o'clock position and continue anti-clockwise.
2. Write the months of the Revolutionary Calendar into the spaces on disc 2. Start at the 3 o'clock position and continue clockwise.
3. Write the years of the Christian calendar from 1792 to 1806 in the spaces on disc 4. Write the years of the Revolutionary Calendar fron Year I to Year XIV into the spaces on disc 5.
4. Using source 23 on page 48 of your book for ideas, decorate the rectangle with information and designs about the Revolutionary Calendar.
5. Stick the whole sheet to some stiff thin card. Cut out the discs and the rectangle, as well as the 'windows' in the rectangle. Pin the discs to the back of the rectangle.
6. Use your model to help you explain (a) why revolutionaries thought this calendar was better than the Christian calendar, and (b) why many French people found the Revolutionary Calendar very difficult to use.

The Revolutionary Calendar

Years — 1792 became Year I. Years were numbered with Roman numerals: I, II, III, IV, V, etc. up to Year XIV.

Months — There were 12 months of 30 days each. They were:

Vendémiaire	(the month of the vintage)	22 Sep - 21 Oct
Brumaire	(the month of fog)	22 Oct - 20 Nov
Frimaire	(the month of frost)	21 Nov - 20 Dec
Nivôse	(the month of snow)	21 Dec - 19 Jan
Pluviôse	(the month of rain)	20 Jan - 18 Feb
Ventôse	(the month of wind)	19 Feb - 20 Mar
Germinal	(the month of germination)	21 Mar - 19 Apr
Floréal	(the month of flowering)	20 Apr - 19 May
Prairial	(the month of meadows)	20 May - 18 Jun
Messidor	(the month of the harvest)	19 Jun - 18 Jul
Thermidor	(the month of heat)	19 Jul - 17 Aug
Fructidor	(the month of fruiting)	18 Aug - 16 Sep

Weeks — Each week was 10 days long. There were 3 weeks in a month. The days of the week were called by their ordinal numbers: Primidi (Firstday), Duodi (Secondday), Tridi (Thirdday), Quartidi (Fourthday), Quintidi (Fifthday), Sextidi (Sixthday), Septidi (Seventhday), Octidi (Eighthday), Nonidi (Ninthday), Décadi (Tenthday)

Hours — Each day was divided into 10 hours. Each hour was divided into 100 minutes. Each minute was divided into 100 seconds.

Holidays — The official rest day was Tenthday. People therefore had a rest day every ten instead of seven days. At the end of the year were added five extra days because 12 months of 30 days each = 360 days, but it takes 365 days for the earth to orbit the sun (366 in leap years). These extra days were called *sans culotte* days and were national holidays.

Do-it-yourself Revolutionary Calendar — Copymaster sheet 4b

1

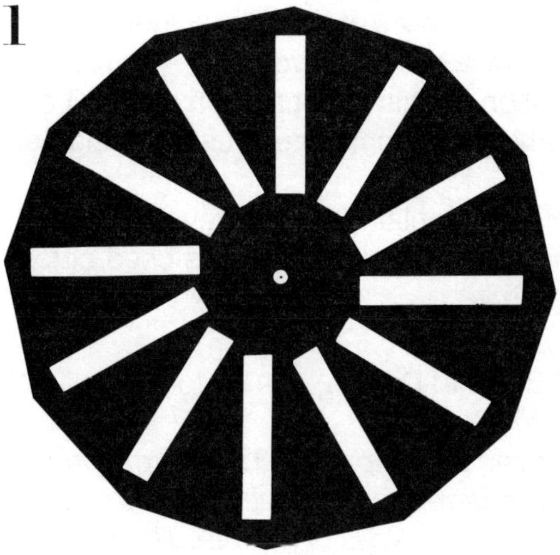

2

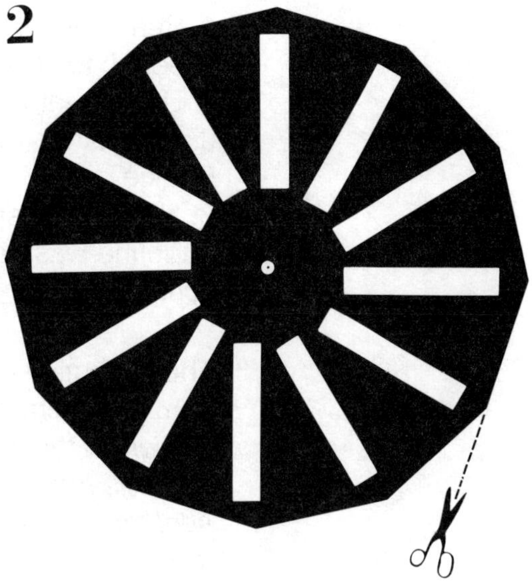

3

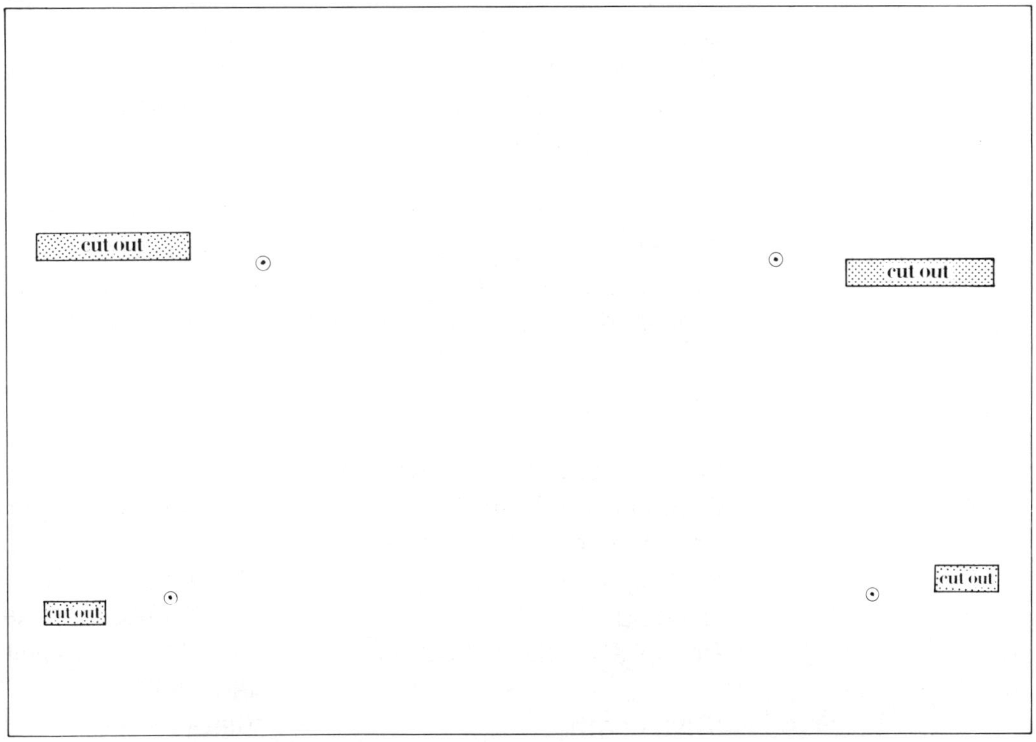

4

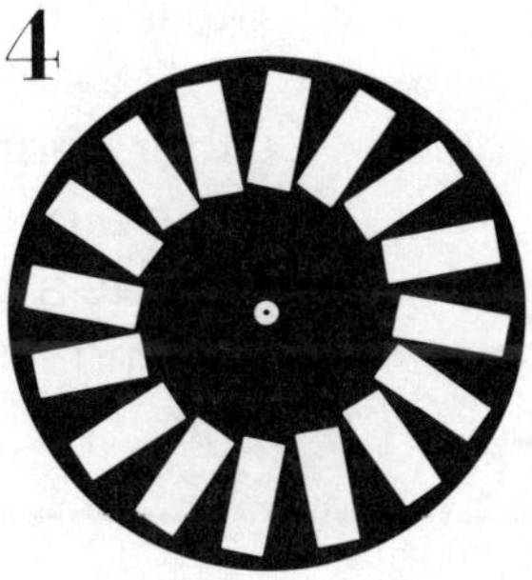

5

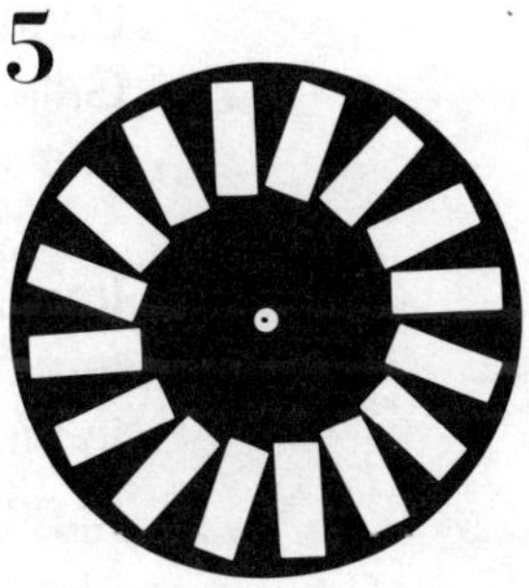

The guillotine

Copymaster sheet 5a

1. Read source 20 on page 45 of your book, then label the picture on sheet 5b to show how a guillotine worked.
2. Use the information on this sheet and on page 14 of your book to display other methods of punishment used in eighteenth-century France.
3. Use your display to explain why the revolutionaries thought the guillotine was an improvement on methods used before the revolution.

The execution of Bernard Dupois, a tailor found guilty of stealing from a church, in 1783:
At eight in the morning of 11 April 1783 . . . the prisoner was released from his irons and ordered to his knees while the officials read the sentence spelling out the details of his fate. The first act specified by the sentence was the . . . rack. The condemned man withstood 23 turns of the device. The rack elicited cries of 'Alas!' 'My God!' and 'Mercy!' from Dupois but he continually affirmed . . . that he had acted alone. When the torture ended . . . Dupois was taken from the jail to Libourne's central square for the public spectacle of his execution . . . There another aspect of his sentence was carried out when the executioner cut off the hand that had offended the laws of God and man by stealing from a church . . . Bleeding, Dupois was taken through the crowds to the gallows where he was hanged by the neck. When the condemned man was dead his body was cut down by the executioner who, in accordance with the sentence, burned the body.
Julius R Ruff, *Crime, Justice and Public Order in Old Régime France*, 1984

Punishments before the Revolution

Capital punishment
Breaking on the wheel (men only)
Burning at the stake
Hanging
Decapitation (for nobles only)

'Civil death'
Banishment for life
Galleys for life (men only)
Life imprisonment (women only)

Imprisonment
In a mental hospital
In the galleys for a set time
In prison for a set time
In a convent (women only)

Corporal punishment
Whipping
Branding (with a V for *voleur* [thief], GAL for galley rower, or a *fleur de lys* [symbol of the king])
Stocks or pillory
The iron collar

Other penalties
Make a public apology
Receive a public warning not to reoffend
Fine

The guillotine

Copymaster sheet 5b

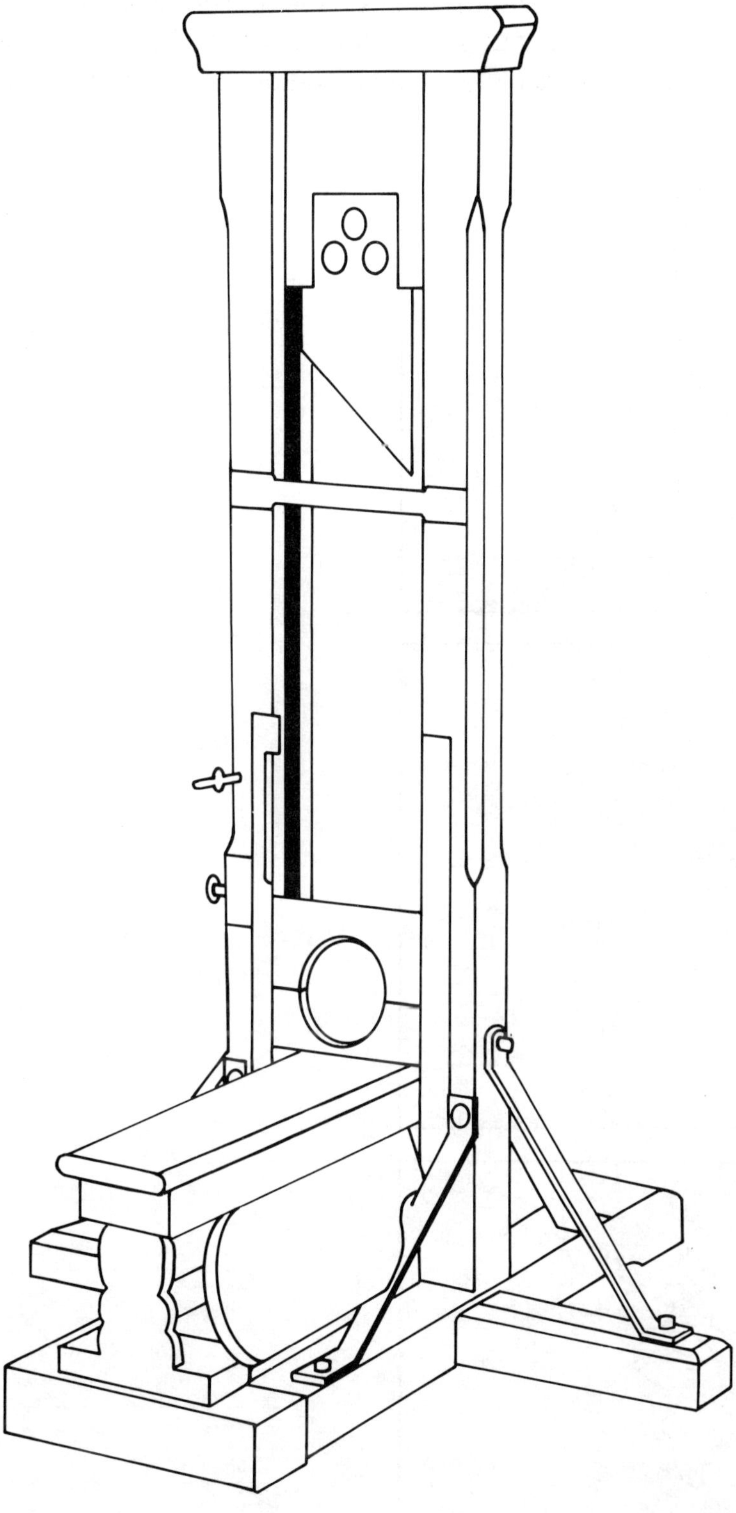

Napoleon conquers Europe

Copymaster sheet 6a

Read pages 67–68 of your book. Use the information to show on the maps on this page and on sheet 6b what Napoleon did in each year to get control of Europe. Show this by writing short sentences beside each map and by colouring or shading the maps and keys.

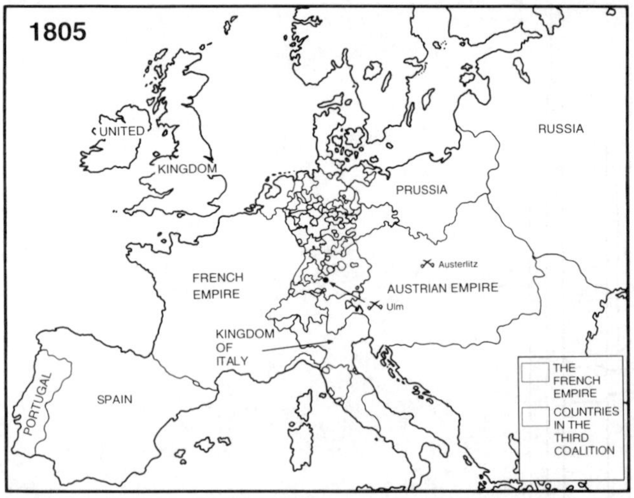

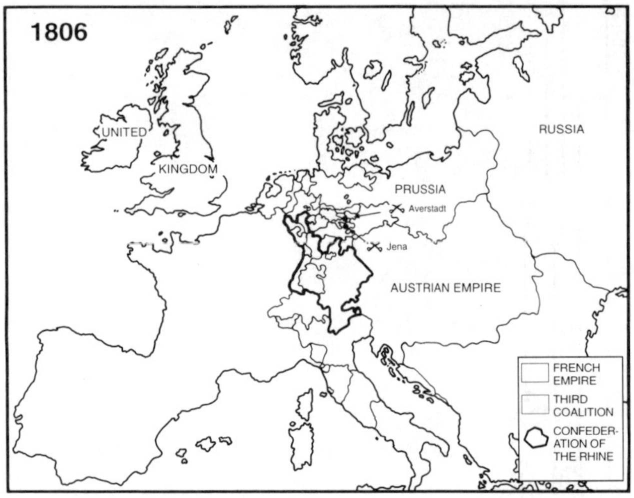

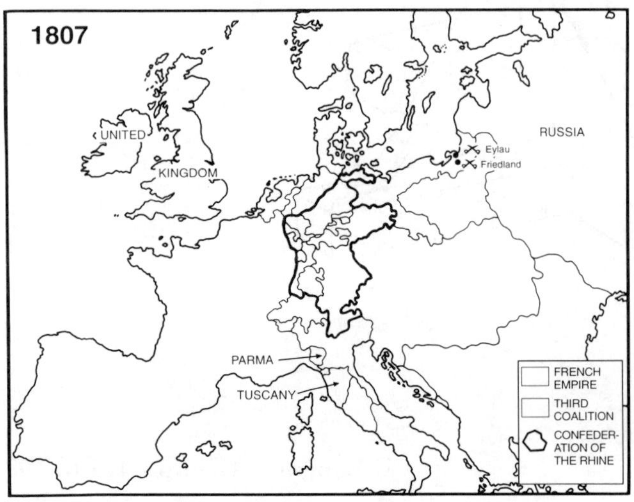

Copymaster sheet 6b

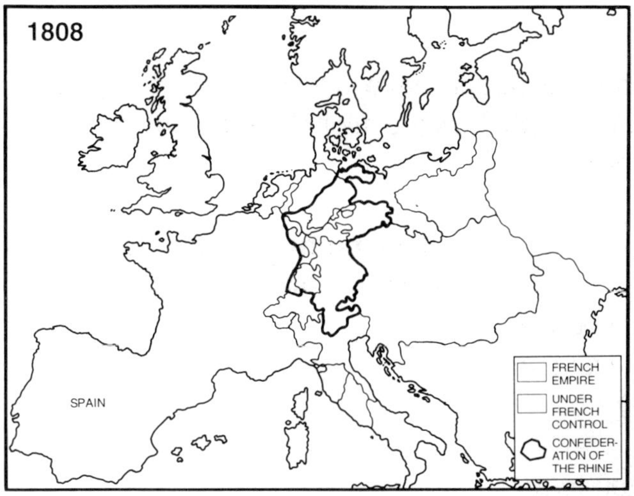

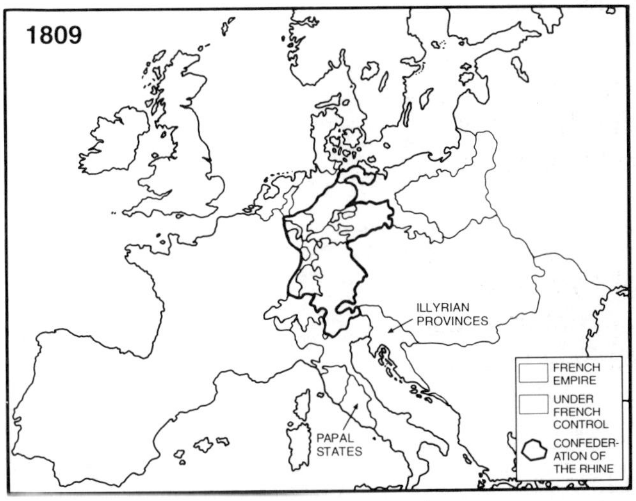

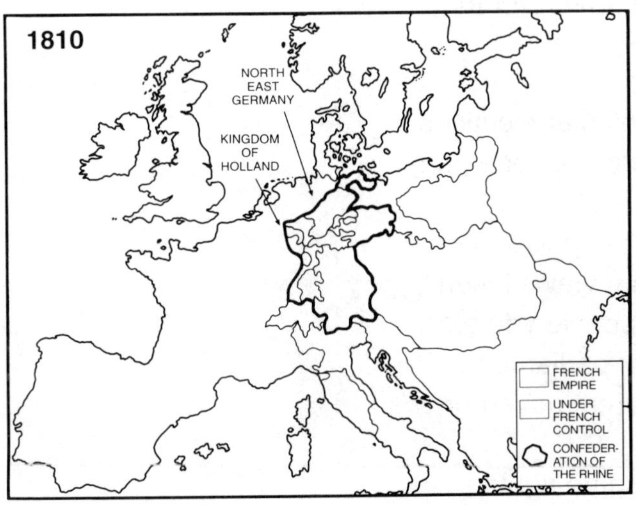

Rights and freedoms — Copymaster sheet 7

The list below shows some of the rights and freedoms that people have in this country today. Imagine that nobody had them. Write down in the spaces on the right how life might be different for you, your family, and people you know if these rights and freedoms did not exist.

Rights and freedoms	What they mean	How might life be different without them
Freedom of speech	The right to say what you think (as long as you don't insult or slander other people)	
Freedom of information	The right to read, listen to and look at any source of information (e.g. newspapers, books, radio, TV, video)	
Freedom of belief	The right to worship freely in your own religion and to hold ideas you think are right	
Freedom in the law	The right to a fair trial if you are arrested; freedom from unfair arrest; the right to equal treatment by the courts	
Freedom of association	The right to join or to form an organisation or association (e.g. a political party, youth group, trade union)	
The right to vote	The right to vote in regular elections in which there is more than one party to choose from	
Representation	The right to have your views taken into account by the people you elect, (e.g. your member of parliament, councillor, school parent governor)	
Equality	Everybody has the same rights	

5 Assessment

The content of *Revolution in France* has been organised in such a way that clear links can be made with the attainment targets. Chapter 1, which is about France before the Revolution, aims to show why there was a revolution in 1789. It therefore leads naturally to questions based on Hi1b: Causes and consequences. Chapter 2 is about the great changes that took place in France as a result of the Revolution, and examines some of the ways in which those changes have been interpreted. Questions on Hi2: Interpretations of history, therefore arise naturally from the material in this chapter. Chapter 3, about the rise to power of Napoleon, puts great emphasis on the ways in which painters created images of Napoleon, and consideration of their paintings allows questioning on Hi3: The use of historical sources. Chapter 4 deals with the changes in Europe brought about by Napoleonic rule, so questions on Hi1a (Change and continuity) follow naturally. Chapter 5, about the nineteenth-century legacy of the revolutionary era, leads to questions about the key features of nineteenth-century revolutionary ideas and situations (Hi1c).

These connections between the content and the attainment targets are intended partly to give each chapter a clear focus, and thus aid comprehension, and partly to make assessment as straightforward as possible. Thus, each chapter ends with a section headed 'Review and Assessment'. The first question in each of these sections encourages readers to review their understanding of the content of the chapter, while the remaining questions can be used to assess levels 3 to 7 in the attainment target linked to the chapter.

This is not to say that each chapter is concerned with one attainment target only. There are questions in every chapter related to Hi1 and Hi3, while substantial sections of chapters 1, 2 and 3 can be used for work on Hi2. And there are questions which are designed either to provoke thought or to aid the reader's comprehension of source material, but which do not specifically relate to the ATs.

The tasks and questions in *Revolution in France* thus fall into three categories. There are assessment tasks covering levels 3–7 of a single AT at the end of each chapter. There are questions covering a variety of ATs, and which provide assessment opportunities at intervals within each chapter. And there are questions designed to provoke thought or aid comprehension but which do not lend themselves to assessment. The grid opposite summarises the assessment opportunities provided by the questions. This is followed by a tentative guide to some of the responses pupils might make to the tasks in the Review and Assessment sections, together with an indication of the levels of attainment that such responses might suggest.

Assessment opportunities in *Revolution in France*

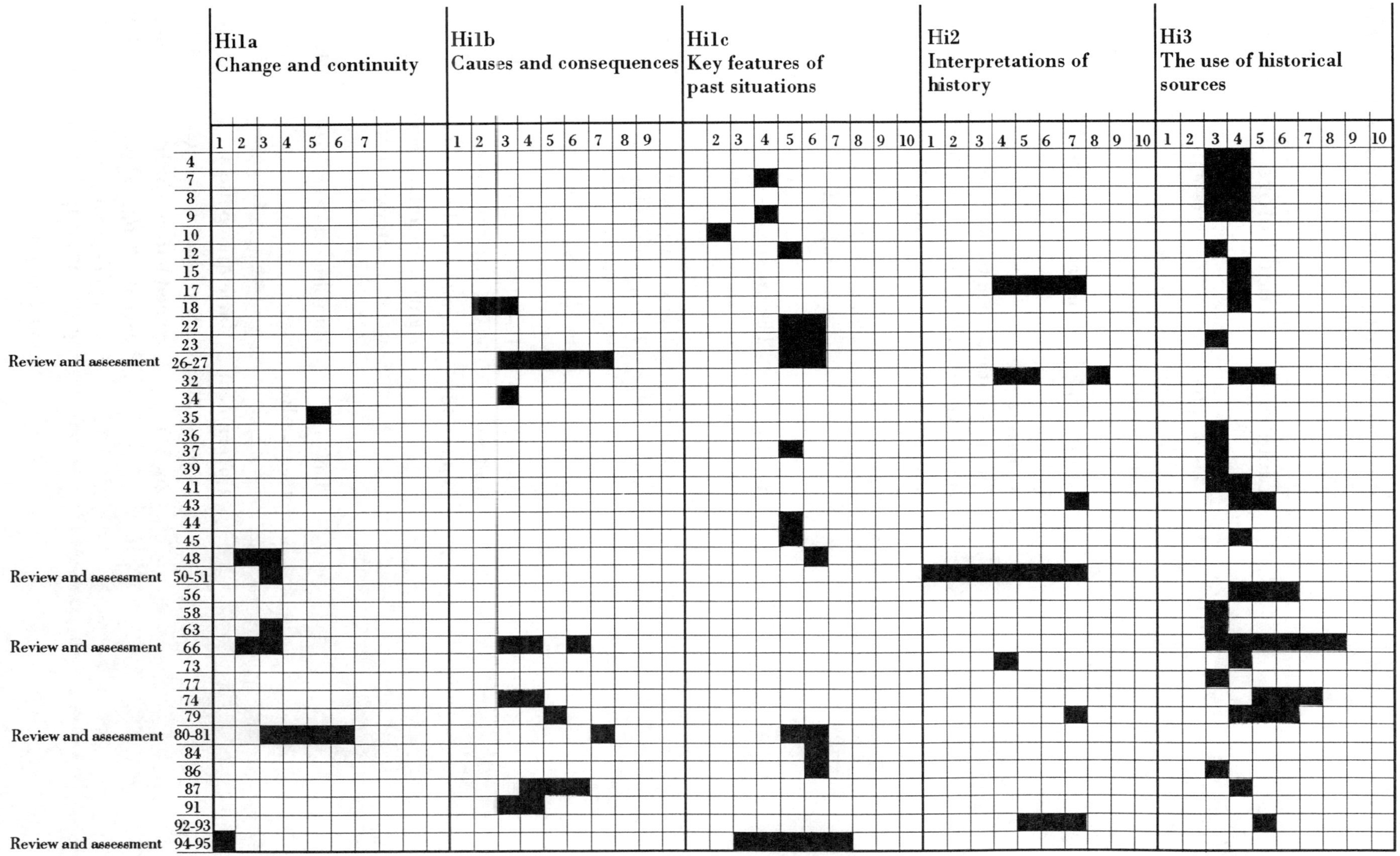

Assessment opportunities in *Revolution in France*

Chapter 1 France before the Revolution

This chapter is about the causes of the French Revolution. The Review and Assessment activities on pages 26–27 are therefore aimed at Hilb: Causes and consequences.

Review and Assessment pages 26–27

Activity 1
This is is not intended for assessment purposes but to allow pupils to review what they have read about the main problems of French society and government before 1789. A completed table might show the following:

	Things that people disliked	Kinds of people who disliked these things
Society (source 6)	The unfairness of privileges	Most of the third estate
Taxation (source 12)	There were many taxes. Taxes were unfair in that some people did not have to pay them	Most of the third estate
Feudal rights and dues (source 13)	Landlords' rights restricted what their tenants could do. Some rights were unfair. Dues were like an extra tax	Peasants
Law (source 16)	Punishments were cruel	Many kinds of people
Government (sources 20, 26, 31)	Marie Antoinette's extravagent spending.	Many kinds of people
	Sealed letters which gave the King and his ministers great power.	People who disagreed with the government
	The exile of the *parlements*	Nobles, third estate

Activity 2
One plausibly identified reason why people wanted change might suggest level 3 attainment.

Question 3
Answers which identify E, B, G, A, I, C as causes, and D, H, F as consequences may suggest level 4.

Question 4
Answers which clearly identify a political cause (e.g. people thought the King and his ministers had too much power), a social cause (e.g. nobles disliked the government's plans) and an economic cause (many people blamed the government for high prices and unemployment) may suggest level 5 attainment.

Question 5
A plausibly identified and clearly explained reason for the government's unpopularity may indicate level 6.

Question 6
Answers of level 7 attainment should (a) show awareness of the role of Marie Antoinette in making the government unpopular, (b) identify at least one other cause of its unpopularity, and (c) attempt to explain that there were several linked reasons why it was unpopular. For example, one reason why Louis was unpopular was because Marie Antoinette wasted lots of money on pointless things like the hamlet. If he hadn't married her this would not have happened. But he would probably have been unpopular anyway because there were other things people didn't like, for example *lettres de cachet*, unfair taxes, food shortages, etc.

Chapter 2 Revolution and Terror, 1789–1794

This chapter has a twin focus: the changes that took place as a result of the Revolution, and the way people have viewed those changes.

Review and Assessment pages 50–51
This section is aimed at Hi2: Interpretations of history.

Question 1
This question is intended to remind pupils of the changes that took place in 1789 but is not intended for assessment purposes. Answers might include any or all of the following:

1 The following events helped to make the French a 'free people' in 1789:

- **A National Assembly was set up.**
- **The Bastille prison in Paris was destroyed.**
- **People in towns and cities all over France set up their own military forces (National Guards) and their own local governments (communes).**
- **Feudal rights and dues were abolished.**
- **A Declaration of the Rights of Man and the Citizen was introduced.**

2 The feudal system was the system in which millions of peasants had to pay money to their landlords and do certain things for them, while the landlords had certain rights over them. It was destroyed in 1789 when peasants refused to pay their dues and burned down their landlords' homes during the Great Fear. This scared the National Assembly into abolishing feudal rights and dues on 4 August.

3 Justice – which means fairness and equality – 'triumphed' in 1789 in several ways:

- **Louis XVI began sharing his power with the people.**
- **Prisoners unfairly locked in the Bastille were freed.**
- **Unfair feudal rights and dues were abolished.**
- **The Declaration of the Rights of Man and the Citizen gave everybody more rights.**

Question 2

This is a level 1 exercise, intended to provide easy access into Hi2. Pupils should have little difficulty in identifying Louis XVI and Marie Antoinette as people who existed and figures such as the winged angel and the goddess of justice as imaginary beings.

Question 3 targets levels 2 to 4

3a is intended to ease access into the questioning. Pupils should be able to spot differences such as:

- The nun's cross in 25 is missing in 26.
- The goddess of justice on the pedestal in 25 is missing in 26.
- The writing about Louis XVI on the pedestal in 25 ('Louis XVI. Father of the People. King of a free people') has been erased in 26.
- The writing inside the arch in 25 ('To the memory of the Estates General of 1789') has been changed in 26 ('To the memory of the French People who conquered liberty on 14 July 1789').

Identification of such differences could be used as evidence of level 2 attainment.

3b is intended simply to provoke the level 3 response that there can be two different points of view about the same events – that the artist of source 26 disagreed with Vangelisti's point of view in 25. Answers which also suggest that the artist of 26 in the year 1800 knew things about Louis XVI which Vangelisti couldn't have known in 1789 would suggest attainment at level 4.

Question 4 targets level 5

There are several plausible answers. For example:

- The changes in 26 were made in 1800, long after the Reign of Terror was over, so the artist might have forgotten how much people's liberty was limited then.
- The artist disliked Louis so much that getting rid of him was more important than loss of liberty in the Reign of Terror.
- Perhaps the artist was being deliberately one-sided in his interpretation because this was meant as propaganda in support of the Revolution.
- Perhaps the artist was scared to show any bad aspects of the Revolution in case he got into trouble.

(It is possible that answers which develop any of these ideas could attain Hi2/8.)

Question 5 targets level 6

Pupils should be able to identify statements A, G, H, J as supporting the artist's interpretation and statements C and I as disagreeing with his interpretation. Sound level 6 answers might show how any or all of statements B, D, E and F could be used both to support and to disagree with the interpretation – depending on how they are deployed in argument.

Question 6 targets level 7

To demonstrate attainment at level 7 pupils will need to use the statements they have considered in question 5 to argue both for and against the interpretation in source 26.

Chapter 3 The rise of Napoleon

This chapter is about Napoleon's rise to power as seen through the eyes of the artists who did so much to create the Napoleonic legend.

Review and Assessment page 66

The paintings featured in Chapter 3 are the subject of the Review and Assessment questions, which target Hi3: The use of historical sources.

Question 1

This is the Review exercise, designed to consolidate pupils' knowledge and understanding of the events leading to Napoleon becoming Emperor. Events mentioned in the chapter which pupils may include on their time-lines are:

- 1796: Napoleon becomes commander of army of Italy and attacks Austrian forces in northern Italy
- 1797: Napoleon conquers northern Italy
- 1798: Napoleon defeats Egyptians in Battle of Pyramids. Following destruction of his ships in Battle of Aboukir Bay, his army is marooned in Middle East.
- 1799: Napoleon returns to France and overthrows Directory. He becomes head of the government (First Consul).
- 1801: Napoleon defeats the Second Coalition. Treaty of Lunéville gives France control of Belgium, Rhineland and north Italy. Napoleon signs Concordat with Pope.
- 1802: Napoleon becomes Consul-for-Life. Reforms French schools.
- 1804: Napoleon introduces *Code Napoléon* reforming the laws. Makes himself Emperor. France becomes an Empire.

(Plausible answers to questions 1b and 1c could also be used to suggest attainment of Hi1/4b and Hi1/5b.)

Question 2 targets Hi3/3

Pupils may deduce any or all of the following from sources 1 and 7:

- Soldiers fought on horseback and on foot.
- Weapons included swords, muskets, cannons.
- Soldiers wore brightly coloured uniforms.
- Soldiers fought in massed formations/lines, etc.

Deduction of at least two may suggest level 3 attainment.

Question 3 targets level 4

The sources all seem to agree that there was a commotion among the deputies when Napoleon entered the Council and that he received protection from guards. They do not definitely show that any of the deputies had weapons or that there was an attempt on Napoleon's life.

Question 4 targets level 5

Pupils should be able to suggest the kind of enquiry in which source 14 could be used as evidence, and then identify features of the painting which can be used as evidence for that particular enquiry. For example, if the enquiry were into the nature of Napoleon's government, the following would be useful:

- his relatives (showing the importance of Napoleon's family in government);
- the Marshals (showing the importance of the army in the maintenance of power);

- the Pope and clergy (showing the importance of the Catholic Church in providing support for his régime).

If the enquiry were into Empire styles, the following would be useful: hairstyles, hats, dresses, jewellery, etc.

Question 5 targets level 6

5a sets up the question. Obvious differences that pupils may note are:

- Napoleon is wearing a scarlet cloak in 9 but a grey coat in 11.
- He has a sash around his waist in 9 but not in 11.
- His left hand is gloved in 9 but bare in 11.
- His boots are shiny in 9 but scuffed and dirty in 11.
- He is riding a horse in 9 but a donkey in 11.
- Napoleon seems to be leading in 9 but is being led in 11.
- There is snow on the ground in 11 but not in 9.

(Close examination also reveals many similarities of detail in the clothing.)

Pupils approaching 5b should first suggest the kind of enquiry for which the paintings could be used as evidence. For example, how did Napoleon cross the Alps? Or, which of sources 9 and 11 is the more realistic portrait of Napoleon crossing the Alps? Answers to the latter are likely to suggest that source 11 is the more useful, because source 12 corroborates the detail in source 11 but not of that in 9. Thorough answers may also suggest that David, according to source 8, had instructions from Napoleon to capture 'an idea of genius' rather than a likeness and the portrait is not therefore meant to be totally realistic – despite the attention to detail suggested by source 10.

Question 6 targets level 7

Answers are likely to say that source 7 is more valuable as evidence than source 1. Reasons given may include any or all of the following:

- Lejeune was actually at Marengo;
- he sketched scenes from the battle to help him paint this large canvas;
- he was a soldier and knew about warfare;
- Philippoteaux wasn't even born at the time of the Napoleonic wars and didn't paint source 1 until 45 years after the battle.

Preliminary classroom discussion about the paintings could also help pupils to make the response that Lejeune's, while perhaps being more reliable than Philippoteaux's painting, is to some extent an idealised view of Napoleonic warfare (for the reasons given in the notes on pages 20–21 of this *Handbook*).

Question 7 targets level 8

7a sets up the question by prompting pupils to suggest that sources 1, 6, 9 and 14 all show Napoleon as calm, heroic, handsome, commanding, clean, important, etc., and that some of these images may be misleading. In source 1, for example, pupils may suggest that he seems too composed and clean for someone in the midst of a battle who has just had a narrow escape from enemy gunfire. Source 6 gives a impression of resoluteness not suggested by source 4. Source 9 may be misleading for the reasons discussed in question 5. Source 14 is not entirely realistic despite the realism of its execution (see the notes on page 21 of this *Handbook*).

Answers to 7b should comment on how the sources throw light on contemporary and later attitudes to Napoleon. This is perhaps best approached after pupils have read pages 92–93 of *Revolution in France*, about the Napoleonic legend.

Chapter 4 Napoleon and Europe

This chapter is about the changes that took place in Europe as a result of conquest and rule by the Bonapartes.

Review and Assessment pages 80–81

These questions relate to Hi1a: Change and continuity.

Question 1 is deliberately broad, and aims to encourage pupils to review both chapters 3 and 4. Answers to question 1a are likely to deal with two basic features of Napoleon's record:

- Napoleon had been a major threat to Britain ever since 1798: attacking the British in Egypt (1798), organising an invasion of England (1803–5), blockading Britain with his Continental system (1806 onwards), and making war on Britain's allies. Could the British really allow such a long-standing and dangerous enemy to retire peacefully in Britain?
- Britain and the Allies had already tried a lenient exile when they exiled Napoleon to Elba. Napoleon's escape from Elba and the 'Hundred Days' that followed, suggested to the British that he was both untrustworthy and dangerous.

Answers to 1b might claim that:

- The reforms made by the Bonapartes in Napoleonic Europe brought benefits to millions of people (the abolition of feudal rights and of serfdom, the granting of constitutions, fairer laws, etc.). In other words, Napoleon wasn't all bad.
- Napoleon gave himself up to the British 'in good faith', believing that he would be protected by English laws.

Question 2 targets levels 3 and 4

Countries that changed were: Prussia, the Austrian Empire, the Italian states, the German states, Holland, France.

Countries that did not change were: Portugal, Spain, the United Kingdom, Denmark, Sweden, Switzerland. (The Ottoman Empire and Russia changed very little.)

Answers which pick out several changes might indicate level 3. Answers which identify countries which stayed the same as well as those which changed might indicate level 4.

Activity 3 targets level 5

Fully or substantially completed tables showing changes in all five columns might indicate level 5 attainment.

Question 4 targets levels 6 and 7

Answers may focus on the reforms made in the states' laws, society, etc. A fully explained answer would contrast these reforms with changes that brought no obvious improvement to people's lives. Answers could attain level 6 or 7 according to the extent of explanation.

Chapter 5 The legacy of the revolutionary era

Chapter 5 is about the ideas of the revolutionary and Napoleonic era and the ways in which these influenced the development of people's ideas and their societies throughout the first half of the nineteenth century and beyond.

Review and Assessment page 95

The subject of this chapter leads naturally to questions relating to Hi1c: Knowing about and understanding key features of past situations.

All five questions have a double function. All are review questions designed to help pupils look back over the revolutionary era they have studied and to detect continuities in it. As well as allowing a review of the whole period, the questions provide assessment opportunities for levels 3 to 7 of Hi1c.

Question 1 targets level 3

Similarities between the two situations, which were 42 years apart, are:

- In both scenes, townspeople are protesting against a royal decision.
- The decisions they were protesting against were similar: in 1788 Louis XVI's decision to suspend the *parlements* (which many saw as defenders of their rights) and in 1830 Charles X's decision to suspend the Charter, which contained basic rights.
- In both scenes the protests are violent, with civilians attacking royal troops.

Differences between the two scenes are:

- The scene in 1830 is a revolutionary one, with fully armed people fighting for a common cause (represented by the flags).
- The scene in 1788 is more of a riot, in which people are using sticks and roof tiles in a spontaneous protest.

Pupils who talk or write plausibly about any or all of these similarities or differences indicate level 3 attainment.

Question 2 targets level 4

If we could have talked to the revolutionaries they might have said things like:

- 'The Charter gives us rights. You have got to defend your rights. Life without rights is no good.'
- 'This is the thin end of the wedge. If we do nothing to stop the King taking away the Charter, he'll think he can do anything he likes. We'll lose all our rights.'
- 'Our fathers and mothers [of 1789, etc.] fought to get us these rights. We must fight to keep them.'

(It is not envisaged that pupils should write in the style of an interview or conversation with revolutionaries. This is not supposed to be a literary exercise.)

Question 3 targets level 5

The most important connections to look for are:

- **Constitutions.** The granting of constitutions in Napoleonic Europe gave millions of people the experience of having constitutional rights. Many joined in revolutions between 1815 and 1848 to get back the rights taken away from them after Napoleon was overthrown.
- **Nationalism.** Millions of Italians, Germans and Poles had the experience of living in national states in Napoleonic Europe. Many fought to regain their national states after these were abolished in 1815.

Question 4 targets level 6

Answers at this level are likely to mention, with varying degrees of sophistication, that revolutionaries wanted such things as:

- constitutions
- national self-determination
- free speech
- equality before the law
- liberty

Question 5 targets level 7

To attain this level, answers would have to mention one or more factors under at least three of the headings.

6 Further resources

There is a colossal and ever growing number of books and other resources on the French revolutionary and Napoleonic era, only a small selection of which can be included here. The aim of the selection is to suggest a wide range of resources rather than provide just a bibliography.

Books

Illustrated books

Richard Cobb and Colin Jones (eds), *The French Revolution: Voices from a momentous epoch*, Simon and Schuster, 1988

Chronicle of the French Revolution, 1788–1799, Longman/Chronicle Communications, 1989

Christopher Hibbert, *The Days of the French Revolution*, Penguin, 1989

General and reference books for teachers

William Doyle, *The Oxford History of the French Revolution*, Oxford University Press, 1989

François Furet and Mona Ozouf, *A Critical Dictionary of the French Revolution*, Harvard University Press, 1989

Colin Jones, *The Longman Companion to the French Revolution*, Longman, 1988

Simon Schama, *Citizens: A Chronicle of the French Revolution*, Penguin, 1989

General and reference books for pupils

Michael Gibson, *Spotlight on the Age of Revolution* (Spotlight on History series), Wayland

Nathaniel Harris, *Spotlight on the Napoleonic Wars*, (Spotlight on History series), Wayland

Anne Millard, *The Age of Revolutions, from AD 1750 to AD 1914* (Picture History series), Usborne
Graham Mitchell, *The Napoleonic Wars* (Living Through History series), Batsford

Literature and fiction

Honoré de Balzac, *The Chouans* (1829), Penguin Classics edition, 1972: *Un épisode sous la Terreur*, 1830 (Out of print)
Charles Dickens, *A Tale of Two Cities*, 1859. Various editions available
Thomas Flanagan, *Year of the French*, Arrow Books, 1989
Baroness Orczy, *The Scarlet Pimpernel*, 1905. Various editions available
Anthony Trollope, *La Vendée: an historical romance* (1850) Penguin Classics edition, 1993

Art

David Bindman, *The Shadow of the Guillotine*, British Museum Publications, 1989
Anita Brookner, *David*, Chatto and Windus, 1980
Philip Conisbee, *Painting in Eighteenth-Century France*, Phaidon Press, 1981
French Caricature and the French Revolution, 1789–1799, Grunwald Center for the Graphic Arts, University of California, Los Angeles, 1988
Jean-Jacques Lévèque, *L'art et la Révolution Française, 1789–1804*, Ides et Calendes (Neuchatel, Switzerland), 1987
Antoine Schnapper, *David*, Alpine Fine Arts, 1982

Places to visit

For schools able to visit Paris, the following are highly recommended:

The Carnavalet Museum, 23, Rue de Sévigné (The main museum of the Revolution, with a large collection of pictures and artefacts)
The Hôtel des Invalides (For Napoleon's tomb and for the Army Museum which has many exhibits on the revolutionary and Napoleonic wars)
The Palace of Versailles (where it all began) and Marie Antoinette's 'hamlet' in the grounds
The Arc de Triomphe

In Britain, there are Martello towers along the south and east coasts of England, built for defence against the threatened French invasion.

Recorded music

Les 19 Grands Hymnes Révolutionnaires, Erato CD 2292-45006-2, includes famous hymns of the Revolution such as Gossec's *Marseillaise, Chant du 14 Juillet* and *Offrande à la Liberté*, Méhul's *Chant du départ* and Catel's *Hymne sur le reprise de Toulon.*

Musique et Revolution, Erato CDs 2292-45005-2. The three compact discs in this set include all 19 of the above revolutionary hymns, a variety of revolutionary songs (e.g. the *Carmagnole* and *Ca Ira*) military and marches, dances, overtures and symphonies by both famous as well as obscure composers of the revolutionary period.

Beethoven's Third Symphony, the 'Eroica' (1804), was originally dedicated to Napoleon but Beethoven, a strong republican, retracted the dedication on hearing that Napoleon had made himself Emperor.

The first performance in Brussels in 1830 of Daniel-François Auber's opera *La muette de Portici* (The Dumb Girl of Portici), about a Neapolitan uprising against foreign oppression in the seventeenth century, caused a riot which sparked off the Belgian revolt of 1830 against the Dutch. Available on EMI 7492842.

Umberto Giordano's opera of 1896, *Andrea Chénier*, about the revolutionary poet who turned against the revolution, is not only interesting as an interpretation of the Reign of Terror but is also a dramatic and tuneful work in its own right. Various recordings available.

Film

From the earliest days of cinema the French Revolution was a popular subject for films. A few of the better known films, in order of appearance, are:

Abel Gance, *Napoleon* (France 1925/27)
Harold Young, *The Scarlet Pimpernel*, (Britain 1935)
Anthony Mann, *The Reign of Terror* (USA 1949)
Sacha Guitry, *Napoleon*, (France 1955)
King Vidor, *War and Peace* (USA-Italy 1956)
Sergei Bondarchuk, *Waterloo*, (Italy-USSR 1970)
Ariane Mnouchkine, *Seventeen Eighty Nine*, (France 1974)
Andrzej Wajda, *Danton*, (France-Poland 1982)

7 About the author

Josh Brooman is a freelance writer and consultant, producing teaching and learning materials for school history. He was head of history at a comprehensive school in Croydon from 1977 to 1986, where he began writing the highly successful Longman Twentieth Century History series. As a member of the NCC History Task Group in 1990–91 he helped to draw up the NCC's consultation report on which the Education Order for history is based, as well as the NCC's *Non-Statutory Guidance for History*. He has written two other books in the Longman Sense of History series, *Imperial China, from the First Emperor to Kublai Khan* and *The Era of the Second World War*.